Really Simple
Adult Coloring Book

Phil Alderson

Colour anywhere in this book
even the cover!

www.reallysimplelife.com

**Dedicated to Evie
you colour my world**

Really Simple

disconnect
turn off your phone, computer & tv

focus
whatever you do, give 100% of your attention

colour
do amazing things to colour your life

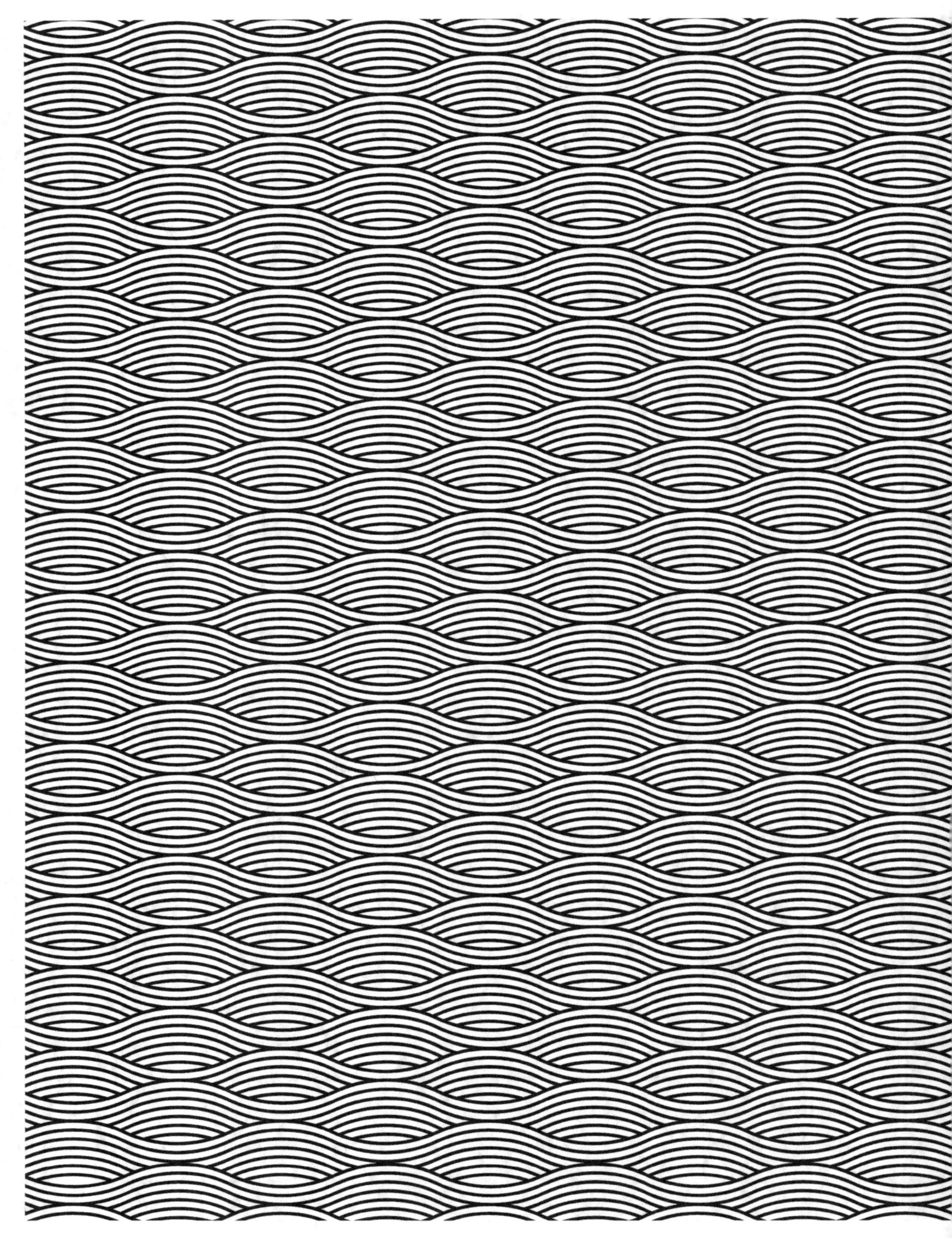

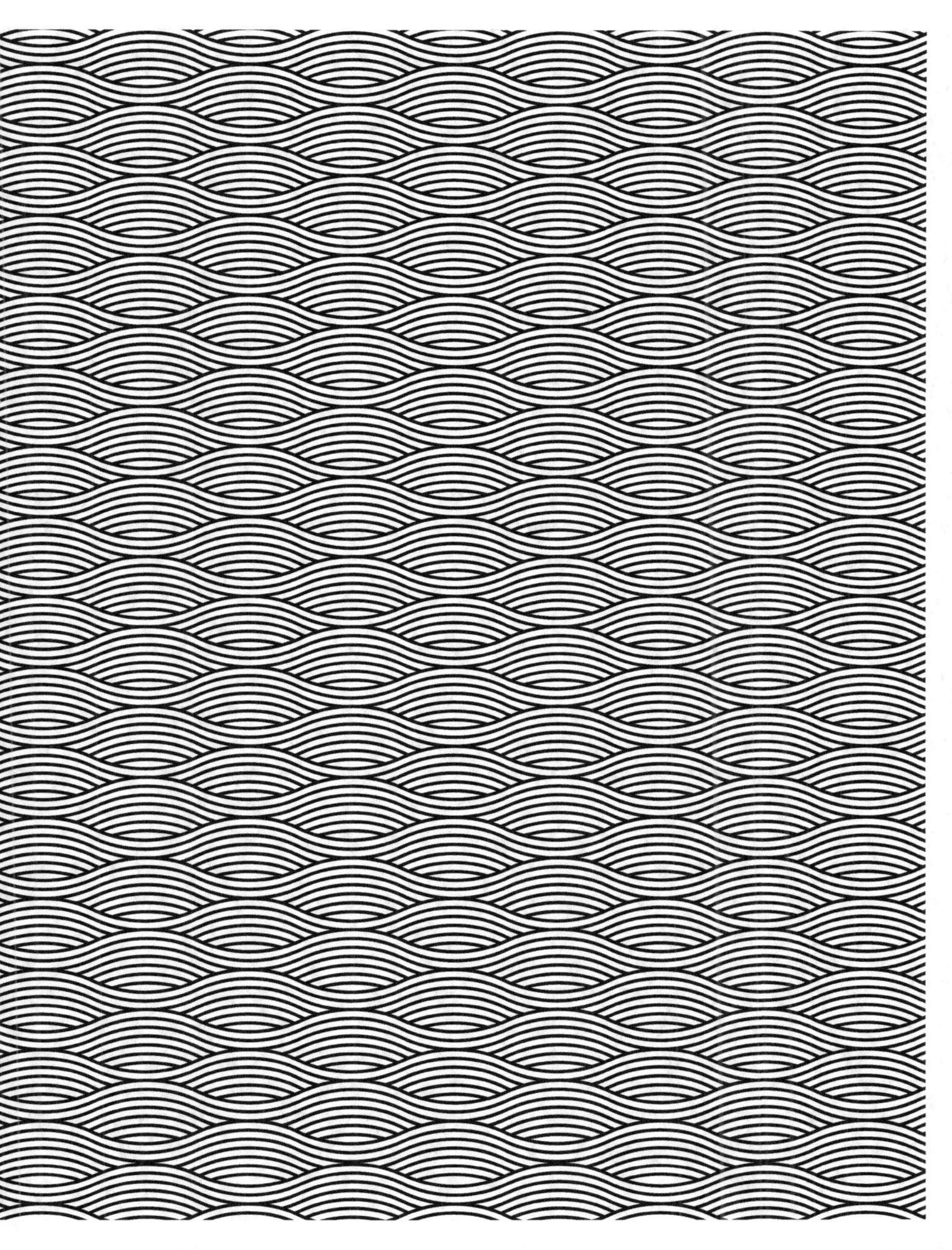

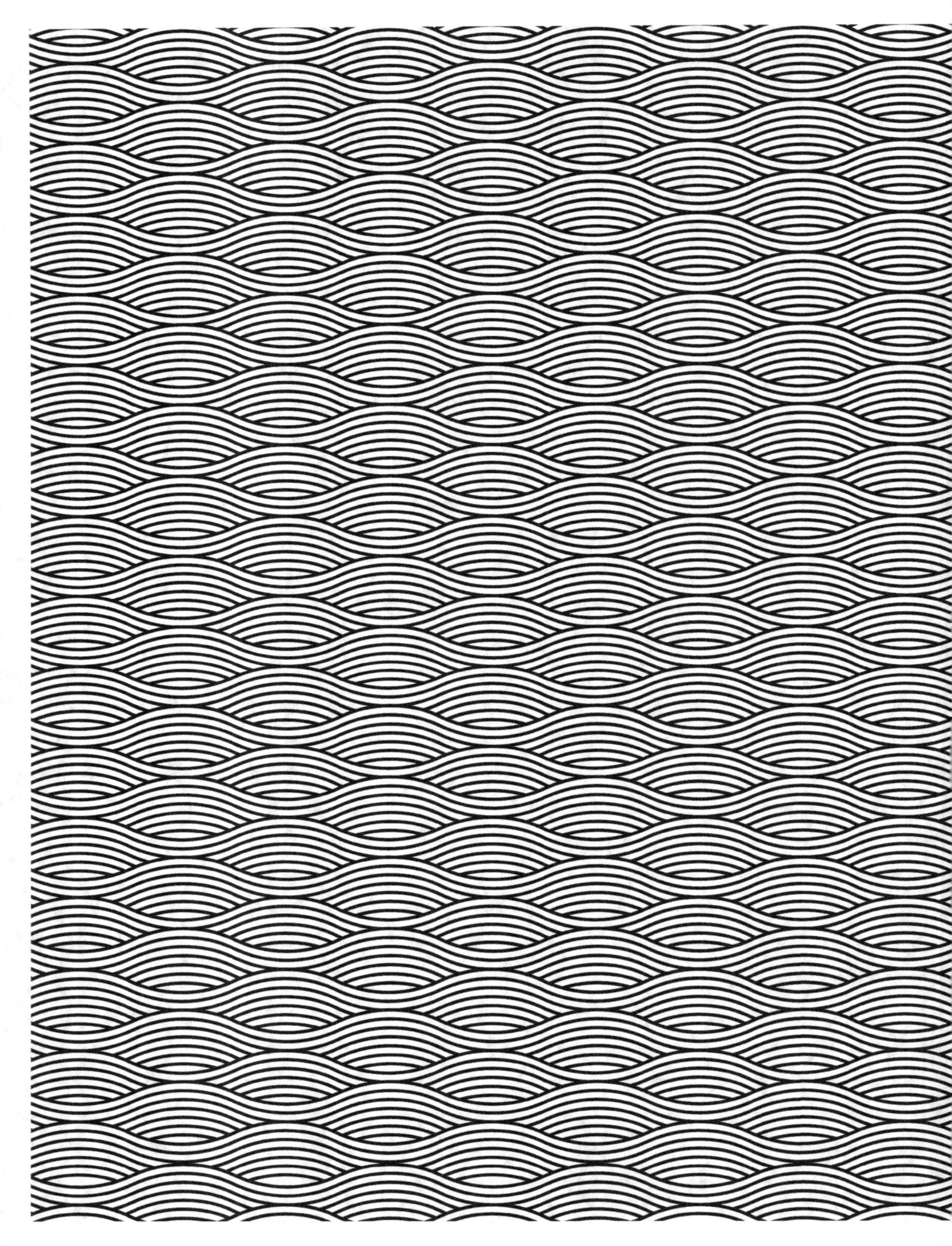

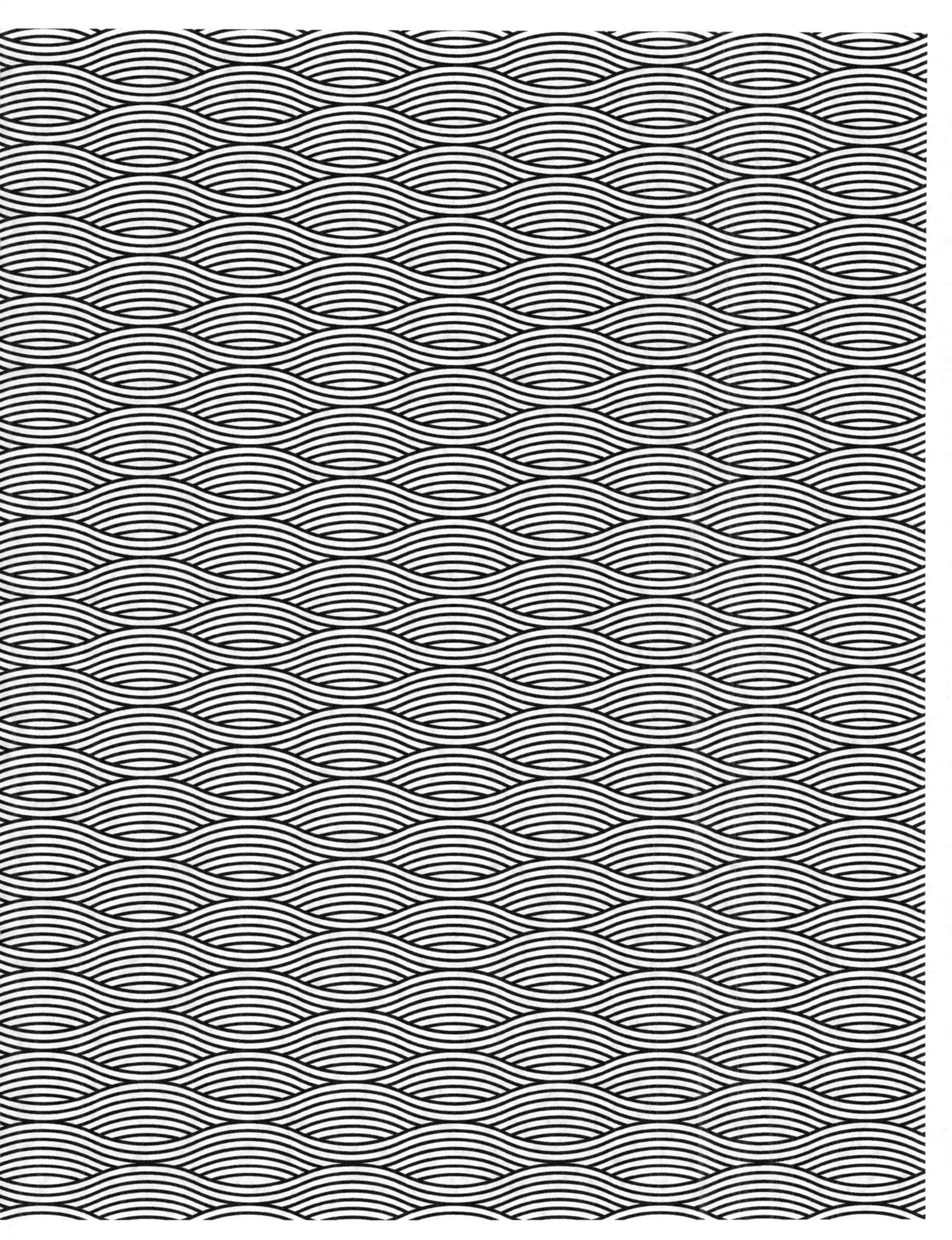

share
#reallysimplelife

www.reallysimplelife.com